Storyboard Thumbnails

16:9 Film Notebook

_____

_____

_____

Scn: Shot: No:

_____
_____
_____

Scn: Shot: No:

_____
_____
_____

Scn: Shot: No:

_____
_____
_____

Scn: Shot: No:

_____
_____
_____

Scn: Shot: No:

_____
_____
_____

Scn: Shot: No:

_____
_____
_____

Scn:	Shot:	No:

Scn:	Shot:	No:

Scn:	Shot:	No:

Scn:	Shot:	No:

Scn:	Shot:	No:

Scn:	Shot:	No:

Scn: Shot: No:

Scn: Shot: No:

Scn: Shot: No:

Scn: Shot: No:

Scn: Shot: No:

Scn: Shot: No:

Scn: Shot: No:

Scn: Shot: No:

Scn: Shot: No:

Scn: Shot: No:

Scn: Shot: No:

Scn: Shot: No:

Scn: Shot: No:

Scn: Shot: No:

Scn: Shot: No:

Scn: Shot: No:

Scn: Shot: No:

Scn: Shot: No:

Scn: Shot: No:

Scn: Shot: No:

Scn: Shot: No:

Scn: Shot: No:

Scn: Shot: No:

Scn: Shot: No:

Scn: Shot: No:

Scn: Shot: No:

Scn: Shot: No:

Scn: Shot: No:

Scn: Shot: No:

Scn: Shot: No:

Scn: Shot: No:

Scn: Shot: No:

Scn: Shot: No:

Scn: Shot: No:

Scn: Shot: No:

Scn: Shot: No:

Scn: Shot: No:

Scn: Shot: No:

Scn: Shot: No:

Scn: Shot: No:

Scn: Shot: No:

Scn: Shot: No:

Scn: Shot: No:

Scn: Shot: No:

Scn: Shot: No:

Scn: Shot: No:

Scn: Shot: No:

Scn: Shot: No:

Scn: Shot: No:

Scn: Shot: No:

Scn: Shot: No:

Scn: Shot: No:

Scn: Shot: No:

Scn: Shot: No:

Scn: Shot: No:

Scn: Shot: No:

Scn: Shot: No:

Scn: Shot: No:

Scn: Shot: No:

Scn: Shot: No:

Scn: Shot: No:

Scn: Shot: No:

Scn: Shot: No:

Scn: Shot: No:

Scn: Shot: No:

Scn: Shot: No:

Scn: Shot: No:

Scn: Shot: No:

Scn: Shot: No:

Scn: Shot: No:

Scn: Shot: No:

Scn: Shot: No:

Scn: Shot: No:

Scn: Shot: No:

Scn: Shot: No:

Scn: Shot: No:

Scn: Shot: No:

Scn: Shot: No:

Scn: Shot: No:

Scn: Shot: No:

Scn: Shot: No:

Scn: Shot: No:

Scn: Shot: No:

Scn: Shot: No:

Scn:	Shot:	No:

Scn:	Shot:	No:

Scn:	Shot:	No:

Scn:	Shot:	No:

Scn:	Shot:	No:

Scn:	Shot:	No:

Scn: Shot: No:

Scn: Shot: No:

Scn: Shot: No:

Scn: Shot: No:

Scn: Shot: No:

Scn: Shot: No:

Scn: Shot: No:

Scn: Shot: No:

Scn: Shot: No:

Scn: Shot: No:

Scn: Shot: No:

Scn: Shot: No:

Scn: Shot: No:

Scn: Shot: No:

Scn: Shot: No:

Scn: Shot: No:

Scn: Shot: No:

Scn: Shot: No:

Scn: Shot: No:

Scn: Shot: No:

Scn: Shot: No:

Scn: Shot: No:

Scn: Shot: No:

Scn: Shot: No:

Scn:	Shot:	No:

Scn:	Shot:	No:

Scn:	Shot:	No:

Scn:	Shot:	No:

Scn:	Shot:	No:

Scn:	Shot:	No:

Scn: Shot: No:

Scn: Shot: No:

Scn: Shot: No:

Scn: Shot: No:

Scn: Shot: No:

Scn: Shot: No:

Scn:	Shot:	No:

Scn:	Shot:	No:

Scn:	Shot:	No:

Scn:	Shot:	No:

Scn:	Shot:	No:

Scn:	Shot:	No:

Scn: Shot: No:

Scn: Shot: No:

Scn: Shot: No:

Scn: Shot: No:

Scn: Shot: No:

Scn: Shot: No:

Scn: Shot: No:

Scn: Shot: No:

Scn: Shot: No:

Scn: Shot: No:

Scn: Shot: No:

Scn: Shot: No:

Scn:　　　　　　Shot:　　　　No:

Scn:　　　　　　Shot:　　　　No:

Scn:　　　　　　Shot:　　　　No:

Scn:　　　　　　Shot:　　　　No:

Scn:　　　　　　Shot:　　　　No:

Scn:　　　　　　Shot:　　　　No:

Scn: Shot: No:

Scn: Shot: No:

Scn: Shot: No:

Scn: Shot: No:

Scn: Shot: No:

Scn: Shot: No:

Scn: Shot: No:

Scn: Shot: No:

Scn: Shot: No:

Scn: Shot: No:

Scn: Shot: No:

Scn: Shot: No:

Scn: Shot: No:

Scn: Shot: No:

Scn: Shot: No:

Scn: Shot: No:

Scn: Shot: No:

Scn: Shot: No:

Scn:	Shot:	No:

Scn:	Shot:	No:

Scn:	Shot:	No:

Scn:	Shot:	No:

Scn:	Shot:	No:

Scn:	Shot:	No:

Scn: Shot: No:

Scn: Shot: No:

Scn: Shot: No:

Scn: Shot: No:

Scn: Shot: No:

Scn: Shot: No:

Scn: Shot: No:

Scn: Shot: No:

Scn: Shot: No:

Scn: Shot: No:

Scn: Shot: No:

Scn: Shot: No:

Scn: Shot: No:

Scn: Shot: No:

Scn: Shot: No:

Scn: Shot: No:

Scn: Shot: No:

Scn: Shot: No:

Scn: Shot: No:

Scn: Shot: No:

Scn: Shot: No:

Scn: Shot: No:

Scn: Shot: No:

Scn: Shot: No:

Scn: Shot: No:

Scn: Shot: No:

Scn: Shot: No:

Scn: Shot: No:

Scn: Shot: No:

Scn: Shot: No:

Scn: Shot: No:

_____
_____
_____

Scn: Shot: No:

_____
_____
_____

Scn: Shot: No:

_____
_____
_____

Scn: Shot: No:

_____
_____
_____

Scn: Shot: No:

_____
_____
_____

Scn: Shot: No:

_____
_____
_____

Scn: Shot: No:

Scn: Shot: No:

Scn: Shot: No:

Scn: Shot: No:

Scn: Shot: No:

Scn: Shot: No:

Scn: Shot: No:

_____
_____
_____

Scn: Shot: No:

_____
_____
_____

Scn: Shot: No:

_____
_____
_____

Scn: Shot: No:

_____
_____
_____

Scn: Shot: No:

_____
_____
_____

Scn: Shot: No:

_____
_____
_____

Scn: Shot: No:

Scn: Shot: No:

Scn: Shot: No:

Scn: Shot: No:

Scn: Shot: No:

Scn: Shot: No:

Scn: Shot: No:

_____

_____

_____

Scn: Shot: No:

_____

_____

_____

Scn: Shot: No:

_____

_____

Scn: Shot: No:

_____

_____

_____

Scn: Shot: No:

_____

_____

_____

Scn: Shot: No:

_____

_____

Scn:	Shot:	No:

Scn:	Shot:	No:

Scn:	Shot:	No:

Scn:	Shot:	No:

Scn:	Shot:	No:

Scn:	Shot:	No:

Scn:	Shot:	No:

Scn:	Shot:	No:

Scn:	Shot:	No:

Scn:	Shot:	No:

Scn:	Shot:	No:

Scn:	Shot:	No:

Scn: Shot: No:

Scn: Shot: No:

Scn: Shot: No:

Scn: Shot: No:

Scn: Shot: No:

Scn: Shot: No:

Scn: Shot: No:

_____
_____
_____

Scn: Shot: No:

_____
_____
_____

Scn: Shot: No:

_____
_____
_____

Scn: Shot: No:

_____
_____
_____

Scn: Shot: No:

_____
_____
_____

Scn: Shot: No:

_____
_____
_____

Scn: Shot: No:

Scn: Shot: No:

Scn: Shot: No:

Scn: Shot: No:

Scn: Shot: No:

Scn: Shot: No:

Scn: Shot: No:

Scn: Shot: No:

Scn: Shot: No:

Scn: Shot: No:

Scn: Shot: No:

Scn: Shot: No:

Scn: Shot: No:

Scn: Shot: No:

Scn: Shot: No:

Scn: Shot: No:

Scn: Shot: No:

Scn: Shot: No:

Scn:	Shot:	No:

Scn:	Shot:	No:

Scn:	Shot:	No:

Scn:	Shot:	No:

Scn:	Shot:	No:

Scn:	Shot:	No:

Scn: Shot: No:

Scn: Shot: No:

Scn: Shot: No:

Scn: Shot: No:

Scn: Shot: No:

Scn: Shot: No:

Scn: Shot: No:

Scn: Shot: No:

Scn: Shot: No:

Scn: Shot: No:

Scn: Shot: No:

Scn: Shot: No:

Scn: Shot: No:

Scn: Shot: No:

Scn: Shot: No:

Scn: Shot: No:

Scn: Shot: No:

Scn: Shot: No:

Scn: Shot: No:

Scn: Shot: No:

Scn: Shot: No:

Scn: Shot: No:

Scn: Shot: No:

Scn: Shot: No:

Scn: Shot: No:

Scn: Shot: No:

Scn: Shot: No:

Scn: Shot: No:

Scn: Shot: No:

Scn: Shot: No:

Scn: Shot: No:

Scn: Shot: No:

Scn: Shot: No:

Scn: Shot: No:

Scn: Shot: No:

Scn: Shot: No:

Scn: Shot: No:

Scn: Shot: No:

Scn: Shot: No:

Scn: Shot: No:

Scn: Shot: No:

Scn: Shot: No:

Scn: Shot: No:

Scn: Shot: No:

Scn: Shot: No:

Scn: Shot: No:

Scn: Shot: No:

Scn: Shot: No:

Scn: Shot: No:

Scn: Shot: No:

_____

_____

_____

_____

Scn: Shot: No:

Scn: Shot: No:

_____

_____

_____

_____

Scn: Shot: No:

Scn: Shot: No:

_____

_____

_____

_____

Scn: Shot: No:

Scn: Shot: No:

Scn: Shot: No:

Scn: Shot: No:

Scn: Shot: No:

Scn: Shot: No:

Scn: Shot: No:

Scn: Shot: No:

Scn: Shot: No:

Scn: Shot: No:

Scn: Shot: No:

Scn: Shot: No:

Scn: Shot: No:

_____

_____

_____

Scn: Shot: No:

_____

_____

_____

Scn: Shot: No:

_____

_____

_____

Scn: Shot: No:

_____

_____

_____

Scn: Shot: No:

_____

_____

_____

Scn: Shot: No:

_____

_____

_____

Scn: Shot: No:

_____

_____

_____

Scn: Shot: No:

_____

_____

_____

Scn: Shot: No:

_____

_____

Scn: Shot: No:

_____

_____

_____

Scn: Shot: No:

_____

_____

_____

Scn: Shot: No:

_____

_____

Scn: Shot: No:

Scn: Shot: No:

Scn: Shot: No:

Scn: Shot: No:

Scn: Shot: No:

Scn: Shot: No:

Scn: Shot: No:

Scn: Shot: No:

Scn: Shot: No:

Scn: Shot: No:

Scn: Shot: No:

Scn: Shot: No:

Scn:	Shot:	No:

Scn:	Shot:	No:

Scn:	Shot:	No:

Scn:	Shot:	No:

Scn:	Shot:	No:

Scn:	Shot:	No:

Scn: Shot: No:

Scn: Shot: No:

_____
_____
_____

_____
_____
_____

Scn: Shot: No:

Scn: Shot: No:

_____
_____
_____

_____
_____
_____

Scn: Shot: No:

Scn: Shot: No:

_____
_____
_____

_____
_____
_____

Scn: Shot: No:

_____
_____
_____

Scn: Shot: No:

_____
_____
_____

Scn: Shot: No:

_____
_____
_____

Scn: Shot: No:

_____
_____
_____

Scn: Shot: No:

_____
_____
_____

Scn: Shot: No:

_____
_____
_____

Scn:　　　　　Shot:　　　　　No:

Scn:　　　　　Shot:　　　　　No:

Scn:　　　　　Shot:　　　　　No:

Scn:　　　　　Shot:　　　　　No:

Scn:　　　　　Shot:　　　　　No:

Scn:　　　　　Shot:　　　　　No:

Scn: Shot: No:

Scn: Shot: No:

Scn: Shot: No:

Scn: Shot: No:

Scn: Shot: No:

Scn: Shot: No:

Scn: Shot: No:

Scn: Shot: No:

Scn: Shot: No:

Scn: Shot: No:

Scn: Shot: No:

Scn: Shot: No:

Scn: Shot: No:

_____
_____
_____

Scn: Shot: No:

_____
_____
_____

Scn: Shot: No:

_____
_____
_____

Scn: Shot: No:

_____
_____
_____

Scn: Shot: No:

_____
_____
_____

Scn: Shot: No:

_____
_____
_____

Scn: Shot: No:

Scn: Shot: No:

Scn: Shot: No:

Scn: Shot: No:

Scn: Shot: No:

Scn: Shot: No:

Scn: Shot: No:

_____
_____
_____

Scn: Shot: No:

_____
_____
_____

Scn: Shot: No:

_____
_____
_____

Scn: Shot: No:

_____
_____
_____

Scn: Shot: No:

_____
_____
_____

Scn: Shot: No:

_____
_____
_____

Scn: Shot: No:

Scn: Shot: No:

Scn: Shot: No:

Scn: Shot: No:

Scn: Shot: No:

Scn: Shot: No:

Scn: Shot: No:

Scn: Shot: No:

Scn: Shot: No:

Scn: Shot: No:

Scn: Shot: No:

Scn: Shot: No:

Scn: Shot: No:

Scn: Shot: No:

Scn: Shot: No:

Scn: Shot: No:

Scn: Shot: No:

Scn: Shot: No:

Scn: Shot: No:

_____

_____

_____

Scn: Shot: No:

_____

_____

_____

Scn: Shot: No:

_____

_____

Scn: Shot: No:

_____

_____

_____

Scn: Shot: No:

_____

_____

_____

Scn: Shot: No:

_____

_____

Scn:　　　　　Shot:　　　　　No:

Scn:　　　　　Shot:　　　　　No:

Scn:　　　　　Shot:　　　　　No:

Scn:　　　　　Shot:　　　　　No:

Scn:　　　　　Shot:　　　　　No:

Scn:　　　　　Shot:　　　　　No:

Scn: Shot: No:

Scn: Shot: No:

Scn: Shot: No:

Scn: Shot: No:

Scn: Shot: No:

Scn: Shot: No:

Scn: Shot: No:

Scn: Shot: No:

Scn: Shot: No:

Scn: Shot: No:

Scn: Shot: No:

Scn: Shot: No:

Scn: Shot: No:

Scn: Shot: No:

Scn: Shot: No:

Scn: Shot: No:

Scn: Shot: No:

Scn: Shot: No:

Scn: Shot: No:

Scn: Shot: No:

Scn: Shot: No:

Scn: Shot: No:

Scn: Shot: No:

Scn: Shot: No:

Scn: Shot: No:

Scn: Shot: No:

Scn: Shot: No:

Scn: Shot: No:

Scn: Shot: No:

Scn: Shot: No:

Scn: Shot: No:

Scn: Shot: No:

Scn: Shot: No:

Scn: Shot: No:

Scn: Shot: No:

Scn: Shot: No:

Scn:　　　　　　Shot:　　　　　No:

Scn:　　　　　　Shot:　　　　　No:

Scn:　　　　　　Shot:　　　　　No:

Scn:　　　　　　Shot:　　　　　No:

Scn:　　　　　　Shot:　　　　　No:

Scn:　　　　　　Shot:　　　　　No:

Scn: Shot: No:

Scn: Shot: No:

Scn: Shot: No:

Scn: Shot: No:

Scn: Shot: No:

Scn: Shot: No:

Scn: Shot: No:

Scn: Shot: No:

Scn: Shot: No:

Scn: Shot: No:

Scn: Shot: No:

Scn: Shot: No:

Scn: Shot: No:

Scn: Shot: No:

Scn: Shot: No:

Scn: Shot: No:

Scn: Shot: No:

Scn: Shot: No:

Scn: Shot: No:

_____
_____
_____

Scn: Shot: No:

_____
_____
_____

Scn: Shot: No:

_____
_____
_____

Scn: Shot: No:

_____
_____
_____

Scn: Shot: No:

_____
_____

Scn: Shot: No:

_____
_____

Scn:	Shot:	No:

Scn:	Shot:	No:

Scn:	Shot:	No:

Scn:	Shot:	No:

Scn:	Shot:	No:

Scn:	Shot:	No:

Scn: Shot: No:

Scn: Shot: No:

Scn: Shot: No:

Scn: Shot: No:

Scn: Shot: No:

Scn: Shot: No:

Scn: Shot: No:

Scn: Shot: No:

Scn: Shot: No:

Scn: Shot: No:

Scn: Shot: No:

Scn: Shot: No:

Scn: Shot: No:

_____
_____
_____

Scn: Shot: No:

_____
_____
_____

Scn: Shot: No:

_____
_____

Scn: Shot: No:

_____
_____
_____

Scn: Shot: No:

_____
_____
_____

Scn: Shot: No:

_____
_____

Scn: Shot: No:

Scn: Shot: No:

Scn: Shot: No:

Scn: Shot: No:

Scn: Shot: No:

Scn: Shot: No:

Scn: Shot: No:

Scn: Shot: No:

Scn: Shot: No:

Scn: Shot: No:

Scn: Shot: No:

Scn: Shot: No:

Scn: Shot: No:

Scn: Shot: No:

Scn: Shot: No:

Scn: Shot: No:

Scn: Shot: No:

Scn: Shot: No:

Scn:　　　　　Shot:　　　　No:

Scn:　　　　　Shot:　　　　No:

Scn:　　　　　Shot:　　　　No:

Scn:　　　　　Shot:　　　　No:

Scn:　　　　　Shot:　　　　No:

Scn:　　　　　Shot:　　　　No:

Scn: Shot: No:

Scn: Shot: No:

Scn: Shot: No:

Scn: Shot: No:

Scn: Shot: No:

Scn: Shot: No:

Scn: Shot: No:

Scn: Shot: No:

Scn: Shot: No:

Scn: Shot: No:

Scn: Shot: No:

Scn: Shot: No:

Scn: Shot: No:

Scn: Shot: No:

Scn: Shot: No:

Scn: Shot: No:

Scn: Shot: No:

Scn: Shot: No:

Scn: Shot: No:

Scn: Shot: No:

Scn: Shot: No:

Scn: Shot: No:

Scn: Shot: No:

Scn: Shot: No:

Scn: Shot: No:

Scn: Shot: No:

Scn: Shot: No:

Scn: Shot: No:

Scn: Shot: No:

Scn: Shot: No:

Scn: Shot: No:

Scn: Shot: No:

Scn: Shot: No:

Scn: Shot: No:

Scn: Shot: No:

Scn: Shot: No:

Scn: Shot: No:

Scn: Shot: No:

Scn: Shot: No:

Scn: Shot: No:

Scn: Shot: No:

Scn: Shot: No:

Scn:	Shot:	No:

Scn:	Shot:	No:

Scn:	Shot:	No:

Scn:	Shot:	No:

Scn:	Shot:	No:

Scn:	Shot:	No:

Scn: Shot: No:

Scn: Shot: No:

Scn: Shot: No:

Scn: Shot: No:

Scn: Shot: No:

Scn: Shot: No:

Scn: Shot: No:

Scn: Shot: No:

Scn: Shot: No:

Scn: Shot: No:

Scn: Shot: No:

Scn: Shot: No:

Scn: Shot: No:

Scn: Shot: No:

Scn: Shot: No:

Scn: Shot: No:

Scn: Shot: No:

Scn: Shot: No:

Scn: Shot: No:

Scn: Shot: No:

Scn: Shot: No:

Scn: Shot: No:

Scn: Shot: No:

Scn: Shot: No:

Scn: Shot: No:

Scn: Shot: No:

Scn: Shot: No:

Scn: Shot: No:

Scn: Shot: No:

Scn: Shot: No:

Scn: Shot: No:

Scn: Shot: No:

Scn: Shot: No:

Scn: Shot: No:

Scn: Shot: No:

Scn: Shot: No:

Scn: Shot: No:

Scn: Shot: No:

Scn: Shot: No:

Scn: Shot: No:

Scn: Shot: No:

Scn: Shot: No:

Scn: Shot: No:

_____
_____
_____

Scn: Shot: No:

_____
_____
_____

Scn: Shot: No:

_____
_____
_____

Scn: Shot: No:

_____
_____
_____

Scn: Shot: No:

_____
_____
_____

Scn: Shot: No:

_____
_____
_____

Scn: Shot: No:

Scn: Shot: No:

Scn: Shot: No:

Scn: Shot: No:

Scn: Shot: No:

Scn: Shot: No:

Scn: Shot: No:

Scn: Shot: No:

Scn: Shot: No:

Scn: Shot: No:

Scn: Shot: No:

Scn: Shot: No:

Scn: Shot: No:

Scn: Shot: No:

Scn: Shot: No:

Scn: Shot: No:

Scn: Shot: No:

Scn: Shot: No:

Scn: Shot: No:

Scn: Shot: No:

Scn: Shot: No:

Scn: Shot: No:

Scn: Shot: No:

Scn: Shot: No:

Scn: Shot: No:

Scn: Shot: No:

Scn: Shot: No:

Scn: Shot: No:

Scn: Shot: No:

Scn: Shot: No:

Scn: Shot: No:

Scn: Shot: No:

Scn: Shot: No:

Scn: Shot: No:

Scn: Shot: No:

Scn: Shot: No:

Made in the USA
Las Vegas, NV
19 November 2021